From the Fourth CCBD Mini-Library Series: Addressing the Diverse Needs of
Children and Youth with Emotional/Behavioral Disorders: Programs That Work

The Challenges of Gangs and Youth Violence in the Schools

Sharon H. Grant
Roosevelt University

Richard Van Acker
University of Illinois
at Chicago

CC
B*D*
Council for
Children with
Behavioral
Disorders

Lyndal M. Bullock & Robert A. Gable, *Series Editors*

The Council for Children with Behavioral Disorders, *Publisher*

About the Council for Children with Behavioral Disorders

Council for
Children with
Behavioral
Disorders

CCBD is an international and professional organization committed to promoting and facilitating the education and general welfare of children and youth with behavioral and emotional disorders. CCBD, whose members include educators, parents, mental health personnel, and a variety of other professionals, actively pursues quality educational services and program alternatives for persons with behavioral disorders, advocates for the needs of such children and youth, emphasizes research and professional growth as vehicles for better understanding behavioral disorders, and provides professional support for persons who are involved with and serve children and youth with behavioral disorders.

In advocating for the professionals in the field of behavioral disorders, CCBD (a division of The Council for Exceptional Children) endorses the Standards for Professional Practice and Code of Ethics adopted by the Delegate Assembly of The Council for Exceptional Children in 1983.

Stock No. D5481

ISBN 0-86586-384-9

Printed in the United States of America

10 9 8 7 6 5 4 3 2 1

Contents

Foreword

In schools across the country, we are witnessing significant demographic changes in the student population. Data show that there is an increasing number of students from culturally and linguistically diverse backgrounds in both general and special education. The long-standing debate over what is special about special education has been rekindled as school personnel struggle to ensure that a heterogeneous population of students receives high-quality instruction. The challenges are many and varied. Concerns about misidentification may have surpassed those of underidentification—especially when we simultaneously look at the numbers that relate to diversity and disability. Diversity is an issue not only in regard to overrepresentation and underrepresentation of students in various disability groups, but also in regard to the delivery of high-quality instruction. There are those who would argue that a limited body of empirical research poorly informs current teacher preparation and classroom practices. Others assert that students who are variously labeled as *emotionally disturbed, behaviorally handicapped,* or *emotionally or behaviorally disordered* are especially susceptible to inappropriate placement and ineffective practices. It is difficult to refute these assertions.

Most education professionals recognize that we must view these challenges as opportunities as well. We must forthrightly address the complex issues surrounding cultural competency, parent involvement in education, high-quality academic and nonacademic intervention, and the judicious use of emergent technology. We also recognize that we cannot afford to ignore the special challenges of serving students with emotional or behavioral disorders placed in interim alternative educational settings or correctional facilities. Rapidly changing social, philosophical, political, and economic forces compel us to examine current policies and practices critically and to repudiate any that do not serve all our students well.

The following books comprise the Fourth CCBD Mini-Library Series: Addressing the Diverse Needs of Children and Youth with Emotional/Behavioral Disorders: Programs That Work, which derived from the 2001 international conference sponsored by the Council for Children with Behavioral Disorders:

- *Addressing the Issue of Disproportionate Representation: Identification and Assessment of Culturally Diverse Students with Emotional or Behavioral Disorders* by Festus Obiakor, Bob Algozzine, Martha Thurlow, Nomsa Gwalla-Ogisi, Stephen Enwefa, Regina Enwefa, and Angela McIntosh

- *The Challenges of Gangs and Youth Violence in the Schools* by Sharon H. Grant and Richard Van Acker

- *Culturally and Linguistically Diverse Learners with Behavioral Disorders* by Gwendolyn Cartledge, Kai Yung (Brian) Tam, Scott A. Loe, Antoinette H. Miranda, Michael Charles Lambert, Cathy D. Kea, and Evette Simmons-Reed

- *Dealing with Behaviors Perceived as Unacceptable in Schools: The Interim Alternative Educational Setting Solution* by Reece L. Peterson and Carl R. Smith

- *Education, Disability, and Juvenile Justice: Recommended Practices* by Robert B. Rutherford, Mary Magee Quinn, Peter E. Leone, Lili Garfinkle, and C. Michael Nelson

- *Integrating Technology in Program Development for Children and Youth with Emotional or Behavioral Disorders,* edited by Lynn K. Wilder and Sharon Black

- *Strategies and Procedures for Designing Proactive Interventions with a Culturally Diverse Population of Students with Emotional or Behavioral Disorders and Their Families/Caregivers* by Gloria D. Campbell-Whatley and Ralph Gardener, III

As series editors, we solicited members of the Council for Children with Behavioral Disorders from across the country to share their thoughts on a range of critical issues regarding students with emotional or behavioral disorders. We are indebted to our colleagues who have so generously given both their time and expertise to making this mini-library possible. We trust that their efforts will contribute to your success and the success of the students with whom you work.

Lynda M. Bullock
University of North Texas

Robert A. Gable
Old Dominion University

Introduction 1

Americans appear to be enamored of violence, as evidenced by the fact that it is a major theme in television, films, music, sports, literature, and children's toys. The media glamorize violence and frequently present it as an acceptable means of dealing with problems. We should not be surprised, therefore, to find that violence is a relatively common phenomenon in the United States. Each year, millions of children witness and/or are victims of domestic violence (Dubowitz, 1986; Straus & Gelles, 1986) or violence perpetrated by non-family members (Lee, 1993). Yet, as children enter school they are often confronted with a so-called zero-tolerance policy related to violence and aggression. These two contrasting standards pose a problem. Children and youths must somehow deal with the mixed messages they encounter related to aggression and violence as a means of social problem solving. Unfortunately, many children receive little meaningful assistance in their efforts to come to grips with aggressive and violent behavior. As children enter school, they must navigate a new social environment—governed by a new set of standards—and deal effectively with any problems that arise. Most children will do fine, but many do not have the social problem-solving skills necessary to address these new situations. Some of these children resort to aggressive and violent behaviors that they have learned elsewhere or have acquired through their interactions with or observation of others.

More than 20 years ago, the safe schools study report by the National Institute of Education (1978) brought to the forefront the grim statistics on violence in our schools. This report indicated that more than 282,000 students and 5,200 teachers were physically assaulted in the secondary schools of this nation *every month*. Since that time, media coverage of youth violence, including the mass shootings in such places as Jonesboro, Arkansas, and Columbine, Colorado, have resulted in a growing awareness of the gravity of youth violence (Lichtblau, 1999). A 1996 national poll of American adolescents commissioned by the Children's Institute International reported that nearly half (47%) of all teens believe their schools are becoming more violent, and 1 in 10 reported a fear of being shot or hurt by classmates who carry weapons. Nationally, over 20% of students avoid using the school bathrooms because of fear of physical assault and victimization in these unsupervised areas (Kaufman, Walker, & Sprague, 1997). The United States Department of Justice (1998) estimated that 1 in 3 youths in the United States will either perpetrate or be the victim of a serious violent crime between the ages of 7 and 18. Youth violence is a serious health problem confronting many other developed nations as well (Hamburg, 1998).

Longitudinal studies of adolescent violence and antisocial behavior provide compelling evidence that the development of such behavior has complex and multiple determinants. However, it is clear that much of this behavior is embedded within the peer group (Elliott, Huizinga, & Ageton, 1985; Hawkins et al., 1992). For example, Patterson (1993) reported that association with deviant peers in early adolescence was uniquely associated with growth in problem behavior. These deviant social networks can take the form of loose-knit delinquent groups or develop into a formal gang. Youth violence is a concern for educational, mental health, and juvenile justice agencies across the nation, each of which provides a range of intervention strategies designed to reduce such behavior and support alternative positive behaviors. The intervention philosophy, ideology, and specific strategies used vary greatly both within and between these various agencies.

In this volume of the mini-library series, we review the current knowledge of youth violence and gang behavior. We examine risk factors associated with the development of violence and the formation of gangs, as well as the functions served by violent behavior and gang membership. We discuss prevention and intervention efforts to help schools and communities identify programs and strategies that have been empirically validated to be beneficial, including school-wide programs aimed at all students, those that target at-risk children, and those that target children and youths who are already involved in violent and gang-related behaviors. In addition, we examine aspects of various intervention programs that have been shown to be ineffective and that may actually exacerbate the display of violence.

A Closer Look at Aggression

2

Aggression is defined as those acts that inflict or threaten bodily or mental harm on others (Loeber & Hay, 1997). *Violence* is defined as aggressive acts that cause serious harm, such as aggravated assault, rape, robbery, and homicide. The type of violence that is the focus of this monograph involves predatory violence, or that which is perpetrated intentionally as part of a pattern of criminal or anti-social behavior and generally results in some personal gain (Tolan & Guerra, 1994). Gang assaults, robberies, and muggings are prevalent forms of this type of violence. While as many as 20% of adolescents have reported participation in predatory violence, only a small portion of this group, 5% to 8% of the males and 3% to 6% of the females, are responsible for the vast majority of these violent acts (Tracy, Wolfgang, & Figlio, 1990). Within the school setting, two forms of predatory violence are most common:

1. *Bullying.* Intimidation, coercion, and threats to safety and well-being are typical forms of bullying. While sometimes displayed toward a target child by a single individual, bullying is more typically carried out by a hostile group of peers (Olweus, 1991). An estimated one-fourth of all students experience bullying, and more than 160,000 students miss school each day out of fear of being bullied (Lee, 1993).

2. *Gangs.* Gangs and gang affiliation, especially in disorganized and impoverished neighborhoods, provide youths with a sense of safety, food, shelter, and clothing. A gang also facilitates its

members' sense of acceptance, belonging, and self-worth. Gang membership, however, greatly increases the risk for both perpetration of and victimization by serious violence (Elliott, 1994).

What leads a child to engage in aggressive and violent behaviors? How do these behaviors serve to meet the needs of the child? How do peers relate to children who display aggressive and violent behaviors? Are there factors that increase the likelihood that a child will join a gang? To answer these and other important questions, we need to explore the risk factors that serve to promote the display of these behaviors and the functions these behaviors serve for the youths involved.

Risk Factors Associated with the Development of Aggression and Violence

When one talks about students at-risk for the development of violence and aggression, the term *at-risk* implies that a child displays or has been exposed to a condition or an event that will increase the likelihood that he or she will engage in serious aggressive and violent behavior some time in his or her development. While a risk factor may predict a particular outcome, the causal relationship between a given risk factor and the outcome is far from clear. In the case of violence and aggression, a number of important risk factors have been identified. The risk factors for the development of violence and aggression are as follows:

- *Individual influences,* such as neurological, hormonal, or other physiological abnormalities stemming from genetics (Cardoret, 1978; Thapar & McGuffin, 1993); impaired cognitive functioning and low academic achievement (Moffitt, 1993); disturbance in the development of impulse control (Loeber, 1991); poor peer relations and poor social problem-solving skills (Parker & Asher, 1987; Selman et al., 1992); and biases and deficits in cognitive processing (Dodge, 1986; Slaby & Guerra, 1988).

- *Family influences,* such as poor parenting and child management practices (e.g., coercive interactions) (Patterson, Reid, & Dishion, 1992; Loeber & Stouthamer-Loeber, 1987); low emotional cohesion among family members (Henggler, Melton, & Smith, 1992; Tolan, 1988); and lack of family problem-solving and coping skills (Patterson et al., 1992; Tolan, Cromwell, & Brasswell, 1986).

- *Peer influences,* such as associations with deviant peers (Cairns, Cairns, Neckerman, Gest, & Gariepy, 1988; Elliott et al., 1985; Gottfredson, 1982); bullying and other forms of victimization at the hands of peers (Lee, 1993; Olweus, 1987); and exposure to classrooms or social network groups with normative beliefs supporting aggressive and violent behavior (Henry, Guerra, Huesmann, & Van Acker, 1998).

- *School influences,* such as classroom management procedures, school-wide discipline policies, and the nature of teacher interaction with aggressive and antisocial youths (Van Acker, Grant, & Henry, 1996; Walker, Colvin, & Ramsey, 1995); instructional practices of teachers (Walker et al., 1995); and the failure to provide instruction and practice related to prosocial behavior (Van Acker, 1993).

- *Community influences,* such as poverty (Short, 1997); neighborhood violence (Elliott & Menard, 1996); social disorganization (Sampson, 1992; Sampson & Groves, 1989); and a community's collective success or failure to maintain social order (Sampson, Raudenbush, & Earls, 1997).

Although considerable research has been devoted to exploring each of these factors, no single factor explains the extent and/or intensity of violent behavior, much less predicts who will engage in such behavior. These behaviors are complex, and only when (a) there is a convergence of a number of risk factors and (b) this convergence involves both individual and environmental risk factors is it possible to predict aggressive or violent behavior (Eron, 1982; Guerra, Eron, Huesmann, Tolan, & Van Acker, 1996; Huesmann & Eron, 1984; Loeber & Tolan, 1992; Tolan, Guerra, Van Acker, Huesmann, & Eron, 1997).

We must be cautious when attempting to identify students at risk for the development of serious aggressive and violent behavior. For many children, experiencing a convergence of these risk factors does not necessarily lead to the display of aggressive or violent behavior. Even in high-risk environments, only a small percentage of youths display chronic aggressive and violent behavior. Apparently, in addition to exposure to a number of the multiple risk factors, children must learn and incorporate aggressive responses within their behavioral repertoire before they can be elicited by some external situation and/or stimulation from within the individual. Moreover, these same children will have had to have failed to learn, or at least not learned as well, alternative prosocial behaviors that could be used in these same situations or as a response to these stimulations (Eron, 1994).

The display of serious aggressive and violent behavior is not limited to children and adolescents of any particular gender, social class, or ethnic group. There are, however, a number of significant risk factors that, in combination, can help to predict risk for the development of aggressive and violent behavior. Individuals with given genetic, neurological, and physical endowments and living under circumstances that put them at risk for violence still vary in their likelihood to behave violently. Ultimately, aggression and violence are learned behaviors. Fortunately, if these are learned behaviors, they can be unlearned.

The Function of Violence

For the most part, children and youths do not simply choose to engage in problematic behavior. They do not select to act a certain way simply to upset others around them or to manipulate a situation. Like all of us, children and youths have needs and, to get these needs met, they engage in behavior. At times, the behaviors they select are deemed inappropriate or even illegal. Nevertheless, these behaviors often serve their desired function. When a child's socially appropriate efforts to meet various developmental goals are somehow thwarted, the child will often turn to less acceptable, but often effective, means to address these needs.

Violent and aggressive behaviors typically serve to meet specific legitimate needs. Far too often, we fail to recognize the underlying need and simply respond to the undesired behavior with harsh and suppressionary tactics that may actually serve to further distance the child from the ability to meet his or her goals. Since the passage of the 1997 amendments to the Individuals with Disabilities Education Act (IDEA), schools have been required to conduct a functional assessment of behavior and to develop a behavioral intervention plan for any student with a disability or suspected of displaying an educational disability, to address behaviors that impact learning and prior to the enactment of certain disciplinary actions. While only mandated for students with special needs, the functional assessment of behavior represents a best practice for all children. An examination of the behavior in light of how it serves the student within his or her social context and how that context supports the undesired behavior provides a wealth of information necessary for effective intervention.

Violence and aggression have been postulated to serve a number of functions (Fagen & Wilkinson, 1998):

- *Achieving or maintaining status.* Within many cultures, individuals, especially the males, must portray themselves as powerful, as someone commanding respect. Physical prowess is often the key to the development of one's self-image. This is especially true in many impoverished areas where access to other forms of status are limited. While there are a number of approved social outlets for an individual to demonstrate physical ability (e.g., sports), for a significant number of youths these avenues appear to be less realistic. These youths may turn to aggression or violence to make an impression on others.

- *Material gains.* For many youths, displays of material wealth play an important role in their self-expression and search for attention from others (Anderson, 1994). Having the ability to display the latest fashions and state-of-the-art gadgets (e.g., beepers, cell phones, jewelry) is a highly competitive and expensive undertaking. Again, for some youths there is a significant disparity between the material goods desired and the legitimate opportunities to obtain them. Efforts to obtain these items may result in violence as the individual engages in behaviors to take them from others.

- *Power and control.* Each of us has to have a sense of power and control over at least some of the events that impact our lives. The ability to influence others and the circumstances in which we find ourselves is thought of as a basic need often met through reciprocal relationships and mutually beneficial social interactions. For some children and youths, these healthy relationships are lacking. Aggressive and violent acts are their only means of control as they dominate others. The violent behavior allows the individual to feel a sense of power and control.

- *Social control.* In any congregation of individuals, there will arise the need for order and social control. In most human societies, rules (i.e., folkways and mores) and formal laws serve to keep order. On the street, aggressive and violent responses often serve as retribution for social transgressions (e.g., slights to one's identity, lack of respect). These transgressions are quickly seen as grievances that must be addressed. Failure to do so would be seen as a sign of weakness. Likewise, violence is commonly used as a means of social control in illegal enterprises (e.g., gangs, drug dealing organizations, other crime organizations). Violence is used to punish violations of business principles or organizational norms (e.g., talking to authorities). In this way, violence serves to keep order and control.

In contexts where the formal social control is deemed oppressive, illegitimate, or unfairly biased, street codes can become normative and take on the mantle of law. Many children and youths feel disenfranchised from social institutions (e.g., family, church, school, community) and hold the belief that they must fight for their own existence and right the wrongs that have befallen them. Membership in gangs and the adoption of their street code provides a sense of order and predictability.

- *Justice or revenge.* Often aggression and violence are seen as a justified response to a wrong. They can serve to provide retribution, restitution, and compensation. To the perpetrator, violence can be held as a moral behavior in pursuit of a form of justice. Much gang violence assumes this retributive form. When a gang member dishonors a member of a rival gang or violates their turf, a collective liability is assigned to all members of the other gang for the actions of the one individual. Gang codes call for swift retribution, often assuming an "eye for an eye" approach to justice.

- *Self-help.* Violence can appear to be a reasonable response to someone locked in an otherwise hopeless situation in which he or she is being victimized. For example, children and youths have been known to commit domestic homicide against a parent whom the child believed would kill him or her or others in the family if not stopped preemptively. At other times, children who feel threatened (e.g., children and youths in violent neighborhoods) may act out violently to prevent future victimization at the hands of others. The individual demonstrates the potential for unrestrained and seemingly unprovoked violence as a deterrent.

- *Defiance of authority.* One of the defining characteristics of adolescence is the defiance of authority as youths seek their own independence. Involvement in aggressive and violent behavior can serve as a means to underscore one's defiance of the social order. This is especially true for those youths who feel the existing social order is unfair.

Examination of the functions we have just discussed suggests that violence may be a very meaningful and effective means for children and youths to meet a number of legitimate developmental needs. Self-esteem, possession of material goods, power and control, justice, self-help, and independence are reasonable and honorable goals. If children are not provided the skills and opportunities to achieve these goals through more socially acceptable means, violence may appear to be a justifiable alternative.

Peer Association and the Development of Violence and Aggression

As we mentioned previously, one of the significant risk factors related to the development of aggressive and violent behavior involves peer relations. Much of the early work in this area concentrated on the consequences of peer rejection (e.g., Asher & Coie, 1990; Coie & Dodge, 1997). The coercive patterns of social interaction that some children have learned at home or resulting from deficits in attention and self-regulation are transferred to the school setting as young children attempt to resolve social conflicts. These patterns of interaction often result in the active rejection of these children. Their early aggressive behavior leads to their rejection, and their rejection in turn leads to greater levels of aggression. These children become marginalized in children's friendship groups, and over time their isolation may become greater. These children may remain isolates or may become associated with other children and youths who support their violent and aggressive behavior, such as youth gangs.

Another approach to understanding how peer relations may contribute to the development of violence and aggression involves an examination of peer social networks. In both elementary and secondary school settings, students sort themselves into networks of distinct peer groups (Cairns, Perrin, & Cairns, 1985; Farmer, Van Acker, Pearl, & Rodkin, 1999; Kinney, 1993). Children are initially drawn to others who share common interests. Typically, children spend the majority of their time with a select group of peers and very little time interacting with others in their classroom. Aggression is one of the characteristics around which young children tend to form peer associations. Children who are aggressive tend to interact with others who are aggressive. Through the processes of imitation, reciprocity, and complementarity, these networks reflect and promote similarities among associates (Cairns & Cairns, 1994; Farmer & Cadwallader, 2000). These processes are defined as follows:

- *Imitation* occurs when one individual copies or models the behavior of another.

- *Reciprocity* occurs when individuals in a social interaction respond to one another with similar behavior (e.g., mutual greetings, escalating aggression).

- *Complementarity* occurs when the behaviors of individuals are dissimilar but are mutually supportive (e.g., bully–victim, leader–follower).

Through these processes, peer associates shape and reinforce each other's behavior. As children affiliate with each other, they tend to become increasingly similar in terms of their behavioral characteristics. As children, whether aggressive or not, associate with peers who display and support aggressive behavior, they are likely to become more aggressive themselves (Henry et al., 2000; Snyder, Horsch, & Childs, 1997). Since the students assigned to various classrooms shift over the years, children and youths are required to continually restructure these friendship networks. Nevertheless, there is considerable continuity in the patterns of affiliation across the years.

Recent research has shown that engaging in violence and aggression may lead to increased social acceptability and even popularity (Rodkin, Farmer, Pearl, & Van Acker, 2000). This is especially true within environments in which there is a greater degree of risk and danger (e.g., inner-city schools). Association with aggressive and violent peers may serve a protective function. Being one of the tougher youths might lead to greater social desirability. This suggests that when attempting to address violence and aggression within the school, we might well be asking a student to surrender the very behavior that leads to his or her social status within the group.

Youth Gangs 3

One type of youth peer group that deserves special attention is the gang. Gangs can be loosely organized groups of youths that often share common concerns (e.g., concerns over territory or turf, sale of illegal drugs), symbols, special styles of dress, or colors. These shared symbols and colors allow gang members to be recognized by one another and by non-gang members as belonging to the gang. Gangs often sort themselves along ethnic lines. Approximately 50% of gangs are comprised of African-American youths (Howell, 1996). Hispanic or Latino gangs, Asian gangs, and Anglo or white gangs are also common. A gang often employs violence as a means to establish status and dominance over others (Gottfredson & Gottfredson, 1999).

In the past, gangs typically were composed of males between 12 and 20 years of age. These gangs operated primarily to afford members status and to provide protection and social affiliation (Vigil, 1999). Gangs were most frequently reported in the large metropolitan areas. Today, more and more females are involved in gang activity independent from an affiliation with a male gang (Klein, 1995). Current trends also indicate that gang involvement is beginning earlier, with much younger members, while active affiliation is now lasting well into adulthood. While gangs continue to bestow status and provide peer affiliation and protection for their members, today they are more likely to serve an economic function—drug trafficking and sales. Presently, gangs are reported to be flourishing in every state in the country. Gangs are found in inner-city, urban, suburban, small town, and even rural schools and communities (Goldstein & Kodluboy, 1998).

Reasons for Gang Membership

Many of the same conditions that lead children and young people to engage in aggressive and violent behavior also serve to make street gang involvement attractive. In a study utilizing extensive surveys of ex-gang members, reasons cited for joining the gangs included availability, fun, friendship, protection, lack of home supervision, having a sibling in the gang, ignorance of the downside of membership, power, control, and status (Spergel, 1995). If a child's basic needs are unable to be met through involvement within socially approved groups (e.g., family, school, community), gang membership may provide a viable option to address these needs.

The correlation between gang affiliation and familial stress is well documented (Vigil, 1999). Many low-income families face an uncertain and insecure future and struggle from day to day to make ends meet. These families often become overwhelmed and, as a result, fail to provide an appropriate level of socialization for their children. When left to their own devices, children turn to the streets for survival. According to Vigil (1999), street children are frequently unsupervised for long periods of time and internalize norms and values to cope with the limited opportunities and extensive dangers they face on the street. Older and longer-term gang members fulfill the role of parent to children from families for whom parenting has become a low priority (Vigil & Yun, 1996), and gang involvement becomes an attractive alternative life-style.

When the family fails to socialize children, this task falls to the schools. Unfortunately, these children come to school with attitudes and characteristics that make school a less than successful experience. They may have irregular schedules combined with a low opinion of the value of education, leading to sporadic attendance and chronic truancy. Due to the lack of family support combined with social isolation, these students may also lack the self-worth and self-discipline necessary for academic and social success in school. In addition, the failure of society to meet the needs of these children may result in a disrespect for authority that is transferred to teachers and administrators and most certainly results in a level of generalized rage against the powerlessness in which these children find themselves.

Like violence and aggression, gang affiliation is related to multiple risk factors and may serve different functions for various students. It is unlikely, therefore, that school personnel can realistically anticipate that a "one size fits all" approach to gang prevention and intervention will meet with success. If a student joins a gang out of fear and a need for protection, the approach to intervention might need to be significantly different than for a student who engages in gang activity to exert a need for power and control.

When serious violence or gang problems arise in schools, administrators have a tendency to respond with a uniform code of conduct—for example, exclusionary (i.e., expulsion, suspension) and suppressive (i.e., detention) tactics aimed at punishing the offenders in hopes of inhibiting the future display of such behaviors (Grant & Van Acker, 2000; Stephens, 1997). In general, this approach has not been found to be particularly effective, and it may actually exacerbate the alienation of students and the display of violence. If a student is attracted to a gang because of a need for belonging, a clear message of rejection by school personnel may make the gang seem even more attractive and justified. If intervention and prevention are to be truly effective, they must remove the need for the student to engage in violence or gang behavior by providing acceptable and effective alternatives. These efforts will typically require intervention that impacts multiple contexts, including the home, community, and school.

Schools Cannot Combat Violence and Gang Activity Alone!

As schools begin to develop and implement programs designed to combat violence and gang activity, they may find that it is a task that requires the assistance of others. Cooperation between the school, community mental health providers, police, and juvenile justice agencies has been shown to be critical to achieving successful outcomes (Hawkins & Weis, 1985; Vigil, 1999). Without an adequate commitment on the part of the major stakeholders in a community, most programs will have very limited success. Violence and gang membership are not simply school concerns; they are community issues that impact everyone. Schools do not fail communities until communities fail schools. Working together, schools and communities can begin to explore the needs of the community and identify current resources, areas of effort duplication, and gaps in the service delivery programs available.

As school and community leaders begin to consider developing prevention and intervention programs, initial thought should be given to preexisting conditions that might lessen the effectiveness of such efforts. For example, schools in which the climate fails to promote social and academic engagement and student success will have a diminished ability to implement effective violence and gang prevention programs. Students confronted with repeated failure have little incentive to become active in program initiatives. They may feel isolated from or rejected by their peers and teachers. On the other hand, if students feel safe, have a sense of belonging, are successful, and feel capable of progress and accomplishment, the need to engage in violent, antisocial behaviors such as those perpetrated by gang members are less inviting. Therefore, as a precursor to the development of a prevention or intervention program, a self-study of school and community settings to identify preexisting areas of need might prove beneficial.

A Self-Study to Identify Needs and Resources

A self-assessment of the nature of the violence and gang behavior that occur within the school and community can help identify needed programs. Schools will need to identify factors within their school and community that may directly or inadvertently add to the problem. The school/community self-assessment might look at the extent of the problem, the level of student alienation, and the extent to which student success is promoted.

- *Extent of violence and gang involvement.* Information could be gathered and analyzed from a systematic tracking and reporting of all incidents of aggression, violence, and vandalism in and around the school. Are there places in the school or community in which violence or gang behavior is more or less likely to occur? Questionnaires regarding feelings of security on the part of both students and staff in the school and on their way to school can prove informative. Reports of whether or not weapons, drugs, or gangs are causes for concern in either the school or the community should be gathered. Teachers and administrators must show evidence of the enforcement of predictable, firm, and fair behavioral standards. This might lead to the self-examination of existing behavior management systems and practices.

- *Alienation and isolation.* There might be a need to determine whether and how various shareholders (e.g., various ethnic and cultural groups, community agencies, parents) are incorporated into the fabric of the school and community. Again, surveys, interviews, or focus groups could be used to seek input from children, school personnel, and parents from all the cultural groups represented in the school and community to determine whether they feel they are treated with respect and dignity. Are school personnel and community leaders sensitive to cultural diversity? Do school personnel, students, and parents feel they are important contributors to the overall success of all students? Are marginal or at-risk students rejected by peers or teachers? What social programs are in existence that are open to participation by all students and in which all students are encouraged to take part?

- *Ability to succeed.* Another important consideration is the extent to which effective strategies are being implemented to ensure the academic success of all students. In the United States, we legally compel children to attend school. Unfortunately, for some of these children, school represents a setting that promotes frustration and communicates failure. Through repeated verbal reprimands for their behavior and comments indicating academic failure, these students get a clear message that school is not for them. Yet we expect these students to return to school each day eager to learn. It seems clear that school personnel have an ethical responsibility to provide a reasonable avenue for success to children who are compelled to attend. School personnel should investigate the extent to which teachers are willing and able to provide the necessary accommodations, adaptations, and modifications to ensure the success of all students—including those who are marginal and at risk. Observations of teacher and student interaction are critical to help determine the need for programs that will allow teachers to "trap" students into academic success. Is student improvement, and not only academic excellence, actively recognized and celebrated in the school?

Once the nature of the existing problems and the preexisting conditions that might reduce program effectiveness have been identified, resources must be directed to address these issues. Thus, another factor that might be important to investigate prior to the adoption of any formal prevention or intervention effort is the resources available to the school or community. This might include an exploration of existing personnel and the way they are being used. For example, one elementary school actively involved social workers and teachers in structured activities before and after school as well as during recess to involve at-risk students in prosocial play activities with their peers. During these times, students are provided direct instruction on prosocial problem solving and are given feedback as they practice these new skills in normal play groups.

In addition, the curriculum should be examined to identify existing opportunities to promote prosocial behavior. Teachers and community agencies should look for opportunities to "double dip" whenever possible. For example, a teacher concerned about the level of aggression displayed by the students in her class could select a book for use in language arts that has a theme of non-violent social problem solving. Thus, she could continue to instruct students in the content of the lesson (e.g., components of the story—plot, setting, character) while also providing opportunities to discuss social problem-solving strategies. This approach could also be incorporated into the preschool and elementary school reading groups hosted by many public libraries. Teachers can program minor social problems into an activity to provide specific students an opportunity to practice social problem-solving skills when the teacher is prepared to provide guidance and feedback.

The opportunities for high-quality professional development and training available to key shareholders in the school and community related to violence and gang prevention and intervention should be assessed. In partnership with community agencies (e.g., police, mental health agencies), schools can host professional and community development seminars aimed at gang prevention and the development of community resilience (e.g., after-school activities, antigraffiti campaigns, strict enforcement of zoning laws, neighborhood watch programs, school-based crisis intervention policies and practices).

Finally, schools and communities will have to determine what financial support exists to fund prevention and intervention efforts to reduce violence and gang involvement and to increase academic success and prosocial behavior in children and youths. Depending upon the extent of the problem and the nature of the programs to be implemented, schools and communities may need to identify federal, state, local, private foundation, or corporate funding.

Identifying the Scope of the Prevention or Intervention Program

4

Drawing upon information from a self-study of youth violence and gang behavior, school and community leaders are able to determine the nature of the intervention(s) they wish to implement. The most effective efforts to develop meaningful prevention and intervention programs make use of a collaborative approach involving a team of educators, parents, students, and community members representing various agencies such as law enforcement and mental health. Using self-study information, as well as current information regarding best practice programs, the team must agree upon the following issues:

- The realistic short- and long-term goals for their program. "What do we hope to accomplish (1) in the relatively near future and (2) as the ultimate effect?"

- The target population(s) for whom they wish to intervene—all children, children at risk for problem development, children and youths who already display problem behaviors, or all of these groups.

- The nature and amount of resources available to direct toward the program(s).

- The number and variety of contexts targeted for change (e.g., student beliefs, attitudes, and behavior; teacher beliefs, attitudes, and behavior; family functioning; peer group affiliation; community services).

- The selection of prevention and intervention program components.

- The monitoring and evaluation of program efforts.

Over the past decade, considerable research has been conducted that can assist school and community personnel as they identify the targeted population, when to begin intervention, and which programs they wish to implement. Schools and communities should seek to select those programs that are designed to address the needs they have targeted and that have empirical support related to their effectiveness. Theoretical advances in prediction and prevention research have emphasized the importance of the interplay between the timing of intervention as related to normal human development and exposure to risk or resilience factors. As a result, information is available to assist us in the better selection of developmentally appropriate program components that are sensitive to the needs of the targeted population.

Is Everything Prevention and Intervention?

At present, there is no shortage of programs designed to help schools provide students with the skills they need to solve social problems, address anger, and prevent the development of aggression and violence, as well as to deter students from gang membership. The National Study of Delinquency Prevention (Gottfredson & Gottfredson, 1997) estimated that during the 1997–1998 school year some 321,500 distinct violence and gang prevention and intervention programs were underway in U.S. schools. Approximately 64% of the 848 school officials responding to the survey on violence and gang prevention and intervention indicated that they had some type of program in place. Unfortunately, the vast majority of these programs have not been empirically tested in a way that would allow schools to have any confidence that they are effective.

While the majority of schools responding to the survey indicated the existence of some form of programming in place to address violence and gang behavior, the authors concluded that many of the programs were weak, failed to implement practices known to be effective, were limited in intensity (i.e., few sessions, short period of time), or provided services for only a few individuals (Gottfredson & Gottfredson, 1997). Most programs involved stand-alone and time-limited interventions targeting social problem-solving or anger-management curricula or assigned students to existing service options (e.g., social work or counseling services). The results of this study led the researchers to construe that, for many schools, everything was thought to provide prevention whether or not it contained the elements necessary for successful intervention (Gottfredson, Gottfredson, Czeh, Wormer, & Silverman, 1998). It appears, then, that many schools wish to implement programs designed to impact the display of violence and gang activity; however, many schools fail to take the necessary steps to design and implement programs that have a realistic chance of preventing the development and display of these complex behaviors.

Empirically Validated or Promising Programs to Prevent Violence and Gang Behavior

Schools certainly hope that the time and effort they put forth to address the serious issues of violence prevention and gang behavior will be fruitful. A number of resources are currently available to school personnel and community leaders to assist them in the identification of programs designed to meet their needs. A number of federal agencies, such as the U.S. Department of Education, the

Centers for Disease Control and Prevention, and the U.S. Department of Justice, provide Web-page information and technical assistance for program selection and development. National organizations such as the Center for the Study and Prevention of Violence in Boulder, Colorado, also provide information on empirically validated program options.

One factor that will help ensure program success is to be clear about the goal of the intervention and the target population for whom programming is designed. Mental health prevention science suggests that programs can be divided into three distinct categories based on the segment of the population that is targeted for intervention. Schools can select to provide programming to all students (i.e., a universal program) or to students known to be exposed to various risk factors (i.e., specified programs), or have programs reserved for only those students who are already displaying violent or gang-related behavior (i.e., indicated programs). In many cases, based on self-study, schools may need to implement programs at each of these levels of intervention. The realities of time and resources, however, may limit the number and scope of programs adopted. Each of these levels of intervention will be reviewed briefly here and examples of model programs will be provided.

Universal or Primary Intervention Programs

Universal or primary intervention programs are designed to deliver intervention to every student in the school or at least every student at a specified age or grade level. Often these programs are aimed at general skill development or the improvement of school climate (e.g., altering the group normative beliefs about the acceptance of violence as a viable solution to social problems). The research on the majority of these programs suggests that they are most effective with children in their early elementary school years (Tolan, Guerra, & Kendall, 1995). Typical universal programs are unlikely to have much of an impact on, nor do they target, students already displaying serious violent behavior or gang affiliation. A number of universal programs that have been empirically validated or that at least show promise based upon existing research are listed in Table 1.

Table 1
Sample of Universal Violence Prevention Programs

Program Name	Targeted Population	Program Description
Bullying Prevention Program Olweus, D., Limber, S., & Mihalic, S .F. (1999). *Blueprints for Violence Prevention, Book Nine: Bullying Prevention Program*. Boulder, CO: Center for the Study and Prevention of Violence.	All students, elementary, middle, and junior high schools. Plus, individual interventions targeted as bullies or victims of bullies.	School-wide assessment and conference to plan intervention. Establishing classroom rules against bullying and holding class meetings regarding bullying. Parent conferencing and individual intervention with children by teachers, counselors, and mental health professionals.
PATHS: Promoting Alternative Thinking Strategies Greenberg, M. T., Kusche, C., & Mihalic, S. F. (1998). *Blueprints for Violence Prevention, Book Ten: Promoting Alternative Thinking Strategies*. Boulder, CO: Center for the Study and Prevention of Violence	Program for all elementary school-aged children grades K–5, including children with special education needs.	Curriculum taught three times per week for 20–30 minutes focuses on emotional literacy, self-control, social competence, positive peer relationships, and interpersonal problem solving. Teachers deliver the curriculum after 2- to 3-day workshop training and bi-weekly meetings with the curriculum consultant.
New Haven Social Development Program Altman, B. E. (1996). *Peacing It Together.* Chicago: Illinois Council for the Prevention of Violence.	All children and youth grades K–12.	Promotes social and emotional development. Includes a social competence curriculum providing prosocial, structured activities. Involves collaboration with a school-based team composed of parents, teachers, and administrators.

Specified or Secondary Intervention Programs

Specified or secondary intervention programs target students who have been exposed to various risk factors that are known to promote violent behavior or facilitate gang involvement. School personnel must engage in some type of screening procedure to identify students who have been exposed to various risk factors or who display specified risk behaviors. Typically, these screening activities require teachers, parents, or other significant adults who are familiar with the child to identify the presence of behaviors that are developmentally problematic. A number of relatively simple screening procedures have been identified (e.g., Drummond, 1993; Walker, Severson, & Feil, 1994). Once these children and youths have been identified, the necessary supports and services can be provided. A sampling of programs found to be effective with at-risk or selected target populations is provided in Table 2.

Indicated or Tertiary Programs

Indicated or tertiary programs involve the delivery of intervention services to students who currently display serious violent behaviors or who are already gang affiliated. Often these behaviors are well entrenched within the students' behavioral repertoire. The goals of most programs at this level are to induce these students into displaying more socially appropriate behaviors and affiliating with prosocial peers. These types of programs are often intensive and individualized. A functional assessment of behavior (discussed in Chapter 9) will help identify the reason(s) a student engages in various violent or gang-related behavior as well as the factors within the social context that serve to support these behaviors. Far too often, the approaches for dealing with youths who display violent or gang-related behavior involve the delivery of some sort of punishment or separate these children from their prosocial peers. Unfortunately, these types of responses to challenging behavior are more likely to increase the probability of violent behavior and alienation and may promote gang affiliation.

Increasingly, schools are developing instructional or pedagogical consequences to address violent behaviors. For example, one high school has developed a partnership with the local police department

Table 2
Sample of Specified Violence and Gang Prevention Programs

Program Name	Targeted Population	Program Description
Quantum Opportunities Lattimore, C. B., Mihalic, S. F., Grotpeter, J. K., & Taggart, R. (1998). *Blueprints for Violence Prevention, Book Four: The Quantum Opportunities Program*. Boulder, CO: Center for the Study and Prevention of Violence.	Adolescents from homes receiving public aid. Grades 9–12.	Small groups of 20–25 students. 250 hours of computer-assisted instruction and peer tutoring to enhance basic skills. 250 hours of development activities for cultural enrichment and personal growth. 250 hours of paid service activities participating in community service projects and volunteering in community agencies.
Big Brothers Big Sisters of America McGill, D. E., Mihalic, S. F., & Grotpeter, J. K. (1998). *Blueprints for Violence Prevention, Book Two: Big Brothers Big Sisters of America*. Boulder, CO: Center for the Study and Prevention of Youth Violence.	Children and youth aged 6–18 from single-parent homes.	A case management approach with volunteers interacting regularly with specific children one on one. Participants undergo an extensive screening process and volunteers are carefully trained. Matches are considered on the basis of needs of the children and abilities of the volunteers. Ongoing supervision is provided.
Aban Aya Youth Project Altman, B. E. (1996). *Peacing It Together*. Chicago: Illinois Council for the Prevention of Violence.	African-American children in grades 5–7.	Afrocentric approach to social development. Includes a classroom-based social development curriculum, development of a school task force made up of parents and other community members, after-school activities, mentoring, and peer mediation; teacher/staff and parent support system composed of workshops and training.

Table 3
Sample of Indicated Violence and Gang Intervention Programs

Program Name	Targeted Population	Program Description
Functional Family Therapy Alexander, J. et al. (1998). *Blueprints for Violence Prevention, Book Three: Functional Family Therapy.* Boulder, CO: Center for the Study and Prevention of Violence.	Youth aged 11–18 at risk for or displaying the development of delinquency, violence, substance use, conduct disorder, oppositional defiant disorder, or disruptive behavior disorder.	8 to 26 hours of direct service to children and their families. Flexible service delivery by teams to homes, clinics, and juvenile court. Wide range of treatment services and service providers focusing on 5 steps: engagement, motivation, assessment, behavior change, and generalization.
Youth Build Goldstein, A. P., & Kodluboy, D. W. (1998). *Gangs in schools: Signs, symbols, and solutions.* Champaign, IL: Research Press.	Out-of-school, low-income youth aged 16–23.	On-the-job construction training with direct supervision and education program emphasizing cognitive skills and application of those skills to the work site. Work on building renovations for homeless and low-income families. Includes individual, group, and vocational counseling.
Gang Peace/First Goldstein, A. P., & Kodluboy, D. W. (1998). *Gangs in schools: Signs, symbols, and solutions.* Champaign, IL: Research Press.	Adolescence through young adulthood.	Health education, substance abuse counseling, neighborhood outreach, youth advocacy, peer counseling, tutoring, and job-finding services, as well as recreational activities.
The Little Village Spergel, I. A. (1996). *The Little Village Gang Violence Reduction Project: A comprehensive and integrated approach.* Paper presented at the National Youth Gangs Symposium, Dallas, TX.	Gang-involved youth.	Collaboration between the Chicago Police Department, community youth workers, and Neighbors Against Gang Violence. Increased police neighborhood supervision and enrichment, including family support, job training, counseling, and other social interventions.

and mental health providers to provide students who engage in fighting or verbal aggression with a 3-day intensive anger management program in lieu of a 3-day suspension. This same school provides classes in dealing with authority and the assignment of an adult mentor to students who demonstrate problems related to insubordination. The classes provide skill instruction and practice of desired alternative behavior, while the mentor provides unconditional positive regard for marginal, isolated, or alienated students to enhance bonding with school personnel. The goals of instructional consequences are to:

- Provide students the opportunity to acquire the knowledge and skills they need to practice the alternative behaviors.

- To provide students the opportunity to practice these skills within a supportive framework in which feedback and instruction are available and are delivered predictably.

Of course, instructional consequences are only a part of the response professionals may elect to implement when addressing the needs of students at the indicated level for intervention. Table 3 lists a sample of programs available to schools electing to target the needs of students currently engaging in violent and gang-oriented behavior.

Functional Assessment of Behavior and the Individual Student

5

To determine which program or treatment plan is most viable for a student who is actively displaying violent and aggressive behavior, a functional assessment of the problematic behavior is advisable. Ultimately, any intervention plan will have to identify how violence and gang affiliation serve to meet the specific student's needs. Armed with this information, school and community programs can provide the student with a more effective way to address the needs previously met through the use of violence or gang affiliation. While the use of a functional assessment of behavior is mandated for students who have, or are suspected of having, an educational disability as a result of behavior, this is thought to be a best practice for all students who demonstrate behaviors of concern.

The functional assessment of behavior involves a thorough investigation of all of the events surrounding a targeted behavior, with the goal being to determine what function(s) the behavior is serving for the student. A behavioral intervention plan is then developed that provides a socially appropriate means to get the need met while eliminating or weakening the path of getting the need met through the inappropriate behavior. In other words, the behavioral intervention plan should support two distinct outcomes: a decrease in the undesirable target behavior and an increase in the use of the alternative response. The behavioral intervention must teach, model, and reinforce the new or more desirable alternative behavior.

The typical steps involved in conducting a functional assessment include the following:

- *Identify the target behavior(s).* This involves generating a clear, observable, and measurable definition (i.e., operational definition) of the specific behavior(s). Members of the assessment team should agree upon the definition so that everyone involved with the child can agree when the behavior is occurring. Most children and youths display multiple challenging behaviors. Team members need to verify the seriousness of each behavior and prioritize those to be targeted for intervention. For example, a student, Brian, may display physical and verbal aggression. These behaviors could be defined as follows:

  - *Verbal aggression:* Verbal or vocal behavior that threatens physical harm or results in emotional harm to others. This includes but is not limited to teasing, threatening, taunting, and name calling.

  - *Physical aggression:* Any physical or gestural behavior that threatens, causes, or potentially causes physical or emotional harm to others. This includes but is not limited to behaviors such as hitting, pushing, kicking, biting, throwing objects, or making threatening gestures as if to hit or throw an object at someone.

- *Collect information to determine the possible function(s) of problem behavior(s).* Existing data are examined, and new information may be collected to identify the exact nature of the behavior and how events in the environment may serve to occasion (i.e., antecedents) or maintain (i.e., consequences) the behavior (Lewis, Newcomer, Kelk, & Powers, 2000). Data may be collected related to events in the environment (i.e., setting events) such as specific physical locations or specific activities, as well as to the behavior of others in the social context (e.g., teachers, peers) thought to influence the display of the behavior. We may wish to examine Brian's school records for information about the history of the aggressive behavior and talk with his parents, teachers, or Brian himself. In many cases, observation of the student in the settings in which the behavior is likely to occur, as well as those in which it is unlikely to occur, can be very informative.

- *Analyze the information collected.* The information is examined to determine the apparent function the violent or gang behavior might serve and how the social context supports the behavior. As a general rule, you will want to triangulate the data. That is, you will want to have three independent sources of data that each support the fact that the behavior serves a specified function. For example, a review of Brian's social history and interviews with his mother and teacher each suggest that he frequently engages in bullying behavior during unstructured times with his peers. He was abused as a child by his father, and coercive interactions appear to be well ingrained in his behavioral repertoire. Direct observation of his interactions with his peers suggest that this bullying behavior is effective, since the peers tend to follow his direction and his aggressive behavior has even provided him a mild level of popularity with some students.

- *Generate a hypothesis regarding the function of the behavior.* Based upon the information gained and the analyses of the data, a hypothesis is generated related to the function of the behavior. In the example just stated, the hypothesis might be that Brian engages in the aggressive bullying behavior as a means to control and influence his peers—a combination of power and control and peer affiliation.

- *Test the hypothesized function.* This requires some care and strategic manipulation of the social context to determine whether the hypothesized function appears to be correct. In our example, we might want to see how Brian behaves if the social interaction is structured in such a way that he can be socially successful (e.g., an activity that allows him to display an existing skill and leadership) without the need for coercion. Does he still need to act as a bully? If he displays more acceptable behavior, we might feel that affiliation and control are reasonable functions for bullying. When he can be successful he does not need to rely on these inappropriate behaviors.

Once the functional assessment is complete, a behavioral intervention plan can be developed and implemented. The behavioral intervention plan is designed to teach, model, and provide Brian opportunities to practice socially appropriate behaviors for getting the previously identified need (function) met. At the same time, it may be necessary to provide a deterrent to the behavior that is currently being employed. The plan should reduce the effectiveness of the current inappropriate behavior while promoting the effectiveness of the alternative behavior in meeting the identified need.

The success of any program to combat challenging behaviors rests on the strength of the procedures in place to promote socially appropriate alternative behaviors. The functional assessment of behavior will typically identify the desired outcome the student seeks (e.g., power and control, affiliation, status or popularity). The student will need to be provided frequent opportunities to both learn and practice the alternative behavior. When displayed, this alternative behavior must be at least as effective, and hopefully more so, than the violent or gang-related behavior(s). Table 4 provides some possible alternative behaviors that could be promoted to serve common functions of violent behavior.

In our example, we might wish to involve Brian in a curriculum designed to address bullying-type behavior while also providing increased opportunities for him to display academic success and leadership skills in the classroom (e.g., through the use of cooperative learning and peer tutoring). Involvement in structured social interaction programs such as after-school recreation programs might also be helpful. At the same time, a simple yet predictable consequence would be in place for addressing instances when bullying-type behaviors are displayed (e.g., response cost, differential reinforcement for low rate of behaviors, use of short time-outs).

Table 4
Alternative Behaviors to Meet Specified Functions of Violence

Function / Activity	Power & Control	Status	Justice or Revenge	Self Help	Affiliation
After-school clubs/sports/structured recreation programs					X
Provide leadership role in class or school	X	X			X
Promote academic success through increased opportunities to respond with appropriate content		X		X	
Provide choices in drill and practice academic tasks	X				
Cooperative learning activities	X			X	X
Recognition for academic improvement not just academic excellence		X		X	
Involvement as peer tutor	X	X		X	X
Leadership role in working with younger or disabled students	X	X			
Peer mediation program—student serves as peer mediator	X	X	X		
Involvement in law-related education activities or programs	X		X		
Service learning activities and other structured activities with prosocial peers	X				X
Empathy and character education programs				X	
Mentoring program					X

Cautionary Notes and Concerns

6

Over the past several decades, hundreds of controlled studies have been carried out to explore adolescent problem behavior. One of the seldom discussed benefits of this research is the identification of programs that actually have negative effects (i.e., iatrogenic effects) on children and youths. Lipsey (1992) reported that 29% of the published intervention studies he reviewed demonstrated negative or harmful effects. This may well be a significant underestimation of the number of such studies due to the reticence of researchers to publish studies with null results, much less those that demonstrate harmful outcomes (Dawes, 1994). Yet one of the important contributions research could provide would be to identify harmful programs so that we could cull iatrogenic interventions from the armamentarium of program options. In this chapter, we will discuss some of the key program properties that have been shown to demonstrate harmful effects.

Grouping High-Risk Students Together for Intervention

As we mentioned earlier, children and youths can significantly impact and support one another's display of aggressive and violent behavior. Singling out for intervention students who are displaying violent behavior or are at high risk for the development of aggression and violent behavior and then grouping these students together may in fact exacerbate the problem. These groupings may serve to support the display and maintenance of the very antisocial behaviors that are targeted for intervention (Dishion, McCord, & Poulin, 1999). Unfortunately, this is a common practice in schools today since it constitutes an economical means to deliver services (e.g., classrooms for students with behavioral or emotional disorders, alternative schools, detention, in-school suspension programs).

Use of Highly Punitive Consequences for Behavior

With media attention bringing school violence to national attention, many community leaders are calling for so-called get-tough policies. Overly punitive programs, however, are not only ineffective, but also expensive. They may take the form of an increase in security and/or law enforcement personnel, the installation of metal detectors, the development of "boot camps," and adjudicating and incarcerating adolescents as adults. Using highly punitive police tactics in the schools may, in fact, put students at greater risk for abuse by school and law enforcement personnel (Hyman & Snook, 2000).

At the classroom level, students who are stressed and angry may engage in disruptive and negative behaviors that, in turn, evoke anger and punishment on the part of the teacher—creating a conflict cycle that escalates until a crisis point is reached (Wood & Long, 1991). At the school level, aggressive behavior more frequently results in punishment and/or exclusion than in treatment and services. While the intent of such measures is to give a clear message that violence and aggression will not be tolerated in the schools, the outcome of punishment is frequently an escalation of the behavior originally identified as problematic. Aggression is often used as a means of escaping punishment or as a reaction to punishment. If maintaining attachment to the school is an effective means of protecting the student from gang involvement and the development of aggression, methods that further alienate and push the child away from the school are ineffective at best and detrimental at worst (Hawkins, Farrington, & Catalano, 1998).

Employing Gang Members or Ex-Gang Members to Deter Gang Affiliation

There is one last comment we wish to make about failed interventions. Following the lead of many substance abuse counseling programs that employ former addicts as counselors, a number of programs have sought to have former gang members counsel students away from gang behavior and violence. Other programs seek to employ peer counseling (e.g., Positive Peer Culture) to help deter gang behavior. These approaches suggest that troubled peers have a level of understanding and credibility that will allow them to be effective counselors with gang-involved youths. The data, however, have indicated that, in general, these types of interventions are more harmful than helpful (Goldstein & Kodluboy, 1998; Lipsey, 1992; Tolan & Guerra, 1994).

Conclusion

7

Violence and gang-related behaviors generally develop as a result of an interaction among a variety of risk factors. These behaviors are complex and are not amenable to simple interventions. Many of the children and youths who engage in violent behavior and those who are attracted to gang affiliation do so as a means to meet one or more legitimate needs (e.g., peer affiliation, power and control, status, material goods). For far too many of these children, socially appropriate means for meeting these needs do not realistically exist. In that gangs and violent behavior serve as effective alternatives, these students have little incentive to change.

The most common approach to addressing violent behavior in schools and communities today involves a zero-tolerance approach that relies heavily upon punitive responses aimed at suppressing the behavior(s) and excluding the perpetrators. While supported by public opinion, these types of responses do little to get at the root of the problem and often serve to exacerbate youth violence. Even when schools attempt to implement programs to prevent or intervene with these challenging behaviors, these efforts often involve stand-alone curricula that are likely to have a limited impact on the behavior. These programs often lack adequate monitoring and support to ensure faithful implementation of even these limited intervention efforts. Any real solution to the problems of violence and gangs will require a concerted and coordinated effort of schools, community mental health providers, and juvenile justice agency personnel to address the underlying factors that lead to and maintain these behaviors.

To maximize the potential for development of effective prevention or intervention efforts, school personnel should engage in a self-study to identify the nature of the problem in the school and surrounding community. Schools will need to implement screening procedures to identify at-risk and indicated students. They will then need to identify community resources that can assist in both identification and remediation of these problems. School personnel will need to seek the assistance of these community resources as partners in efforts to address youth violence and gang involvement. Prevention and intervention efforts should be identified from among those known to have empirically validated effectiveness. Programs should be comprehensive rather than piece-meal efforts. The establishment of multiyear programs that span the developmental years (i.e., solid community-based early childhood programs to support families, as well as primary through secondary school programs) should be the goal of the school and community efforts. Programs can be developed at various levels of intervention to target all students (i.e., universal programs), at-risk students (i.e., specified programs), and/or students who are already displaying violent and gang-related behaviors (i.e., indicated programs). Ultimately, school personnel will need to meet the specific needs of indicated students. The use of functional assessments of behavior to develop behavioral intervention plans that weaken the effectiveness of the violent behavior and promote the use of alternative prosocial behaviors has been suggested.

The task is not easy. Time, money, and effort must be directed to both prevention and intervention. Unfortunately, our failure to respond with effective programming will likely result in outcomes that require an even greater expenditure of resources and an increased number of damaged and angry children and ultimately dangerous adults.

References

Anderson, E. (1994, May). Code of the streets. *The Atlantic Monthly,* pp. 81–94.

Asher, S. R., & Coie, J. D. (1990). *Peer rejection in childhood.* Cambridge, England: Cambridge University Press

Cairns, R. B., & Cairns, B. D. (1994). *Lifelines and risks: Pathways of youth in our time.* New York: Harvester Wheatsheaf.

Cairns, R. B., Cairns, B. D., Neckerman, H. J., Gest, S., & Gariepy, J. L. (1988). Social networks and aggressive behavior: Peer support or peer rejection? *Developmental Psychology, 24,* 815–823.

Cairns, R. B., Perrin, J. E., & Cairns, B. D. (1985). Social structure and social cognition in early adolescence: Affiliative patterns. *Journal of Early Adolescence, 5,* 339–355.

Cardoret, R .J. (1978). Psychopathology in adopted-away offspring of biological parents with antisocial behavior. *Archives of General Psychiatry, 35,* 176–184.

Children's Institute International. (1996). *Armed and Ready for School.* Los Angeles: Pacific Visions Communication.

Coie, J. D., & Dodge, K. A. (1997). Aggression and antisocial behavior. In W. Damon (Series Ed.) and N. Eisenberg (Vol. Ed.), *Handbook of child psychology: Vol. 3. Social, emotional, and personality development* (5th ed., pp. 779–862). New York: Wiley.

Dawes, R. M. (1994). *House of cards: Psychology and psychotherapy built on myth.* New York: Free Press.

Dishion, T. J., McCord, J., & Poulin, F. (1999). When interventions harm: Peer groups and problem behavior. *American Psychologist, 54,* 755–764.

Dodge, K. (1986). A social information processing model of social competence in children. In M. Perlmutter (Ed.), *Minnesota symposium on child psychology* (pp. 77–125). Hillsdale, NJ: Erlbaum.

Drummond, T. (1993). The Student Risk Screening Scale (SRSS). Grants Pass, OR: Josephine County Mental Health Program.

Dubowitz, H. (*1986*). *Child maltreatment in the United States: Etiology, impact, and prevention.* (Background paper prepared for the Congress of the United States, Office of Technology Assessment).

Elliott, D. S. (1994). *Youth violence: An overview.* Boulder CO: Center for the Study and Prevention of Violence.

Elliott, D. S., Huizinga, D., & Ageton, S. S. (1985). *Explaining delinquency and drug use.* Beverly Hills, CA: Sage.

Elliott, D., & Menard, S. (1996). *Delinquent friends and delinquent behavior: Temporal and developmental patterns.* New York: Cambridge University Press

Eron, L. D. (1982). Parent–child interaction, television violence and aggression of children. *American Psychologist, 37,* 197–211.

Eron, L. D. (1994, August). *Aggression is learned behavior and therefore can be unlearned.* Paper presented at the American Psychological Association Scientific Weekend, Washington, DC.

Fagen, J., & Wilkinson, D. L. (1998). Social contexts and functions of adolescent violence. In D. S. Elliott, B. A. Hamburg, & K. R. Williams, *Violence in American schools.* Cambridge, England: Cambridge University Press

Farmer, T. W., & Cadwallader, T. W. (2000). Social interactions and peer support for problem behavior. *Preventing School Failure, 44,* 105–109.

Farmer, T. W., Van Acker, R., Pearl, R., & Rodkin, P. C. (1999). Social networks and peer assessed problem behavior in elementary classrooms: Students with and without disabilities. *Remedial and Special Education, 20,* 244–256.

Goldstein, A. P., & Kodluboy, D. W. (1998). *Gangs in schools: Signs, symbols, and solutions.* Champaign, IL: Research Press.

Gottfredson, G. D. (1982). *The School Action Effectiveness Study: First interim report* (Rep. No. 325). Baltimore: Johns Hopkins University, Center for Social Organization of Schools. (ERIC Document Reproduction Service No. ED 222 835)

Gottfredson, G. D., & Gottfredson, D. C. (1999, July). *Survey of school-based gang prevention and intervention programs: Preliminary findings.* Paper presented at the National Youth Gang Symposium, Las Vegas, NV. (ERIC Document Reproduction Service No. ED 432 652)

Gottfredson, D. C., Gottfredson, G. D., Czeh, E. R., Wormer, S. C., & Silverman, R. (1998, November). *Everything is prevention.* Paper presented at the annual meeting of the American Society of Criminology, Washington DC.

Grant, S. H., & Van Acker, R. (2000). Do schools teach aggression? Recognizing and retooling the interactions that lead students to aggression. *Reaching Today's Youth, 5,* 27–32.

Guerra, N. G., Eron, L. D., Huesmann, L. R., Tolan, P. H., & Van Acker, R. (1996). A cognitive/ecological approach to the prevention and mitigation of violence and aggression in inner-city youth. In K. Bjorkquist and D. P. Fry (Eds.), *Styles of conflict resolution: Models and applications from around the world.* New York: Academic Press.

Guerra, N. G., & Slaby, R. G. (1990). Cognitive mediators of aggression in adolescent offenders: II. Interventions. *Developmental Psychology, 26,* 269–277.

Hamburg, M. A. (1998). Youth violence is a public health concern. In D. S. Elliott, B. A. Hamburg, & K. R. Williams, *Violence in American schools* (pp. 31–54). Cambridge, England: Cambridge University Press.

Hawkins, J. D., Catalano, R. F., Morrison, D. M., O'Donnell, J., Abbott, R. D., & Day, L. E. (1992). The Seattle Social Development Project: Effects of the first four years on protective factors and problem behaviors. In J. McCord & R. Tremblay (Eds.), *The prevention of antisocial behavior in children* (pp. 139–161). New York: Guilford.

Hawkins, J. D., Farrington, D. P., & Catalano, R. F. (1998). Reducing violence through the schools. In D. S. Elliott, B. A. Hamburg, & K. R. Williams (Eds.), *Violence in American schools: A new perspective* (pp. 188–216). Cambridge, England: Cambridge University Press.

Hawkins, J. D., & Weis, J. G. (1985). The social development model: An integrated approach to delinquency prevention. *Journal of Primary Prevention, 6,* 73–97.

Henggler, S. W., Melton, G. B., & Smith, L. A. (1992). Family preservation using multi-systemic therapy: An effective alternative to incarcerating serious juvenile offenders. *Journal of Consulting and Clinical Psychology, 60,* 953–961.

Henry, D., Guerra, N. G., Huesmann, L. R., & Van Acker, R. (2000). Descriptive and injunctive norms for aggression in urban elementary school classrooms. *American Journal of Community Psychology, 68,* 121–136.

Howell, J.C. (1996). *Youth gangs in the United States: An overview.* (Draft report to the National Youth Gang Center). Washington, DC: U.S. Office of Juvenile Justice and Delinquency Prevention.

Huesmann, L. R., & Eron, L. D. (1984). Cognitive processes and the persistence of aggressive behavior. *Aggressive Behavior, 10,* 243–251.

Hyman, I. A., & Snook, P. A. (2000, March). *Dangerous schools / dangerous students: Defining and assessing student alienation syndrome.* Paper presented at the National Association of School Psychologists Annual Convention and Exposition. New Orleans, LA.

Kaufman, M. J., Walker, H. M., & Sprague, J. (1997, August). *Translating research on safe and violence free schools into effective practices.* Paper presented at the Institute on Violence and Destructive Behavior, Eugene, OR.

Kinney, D. A. (1993). From nerds to normals: The recovery of identity among adolescents from middle school to high school. *Sociology of Education, 66,* 21–40.

Klein, M. (1995). *The American street gang.* New York: Oxford University Press.

Lee, J. (1993). *Facing the fire: Experiencing and expressing anger appropriately.* New York: Bantum.

Lewis, T. J., Newcomer, L., Kelk, M., & Powers, L. (2000). One youth at a time: Addressing aggression and violence through individual systems of positive behavioral support. *Reaching Today's Youth, 5,* 37–41.

Lichtblau, E. (1999, October 18). Juvenile crime rate continues to decrease. *Register Guard,* pp. 1A, 12A.

Lipsey, M. W. (1992). Juvenile delinquency treatment: A meta-analytic inquiry into the variability of effects. In T. D. Cook, H. Cooper, D. S. Corday, H. Hartmann, L. V. Hedges, R. J. Light, T. A. Louis, & F. Musteller (Eds.), *Meta-analysis for explanation: A casebook* (pp. 83–125). New York: Russell Sage.

Loeber, R. (1991). Antisocial behavior: More enduring than changeable? *Journal of the American Academy of Child and Adolescent Psychiatry, 31,* 393–397.

Loeber, R., & Hay, D. (1997). The key issues in the development of aggression and violence from childhood to early adulthood. *Annual Review of Psychology, 48,* 371–410.

Loeber, R., & Stouthamer-Loeber, M. (1987). The prediction of delinquency. In H. C. Quay (Ed.), *Handbook of juvenile delinquency* (pp. 325–382). New York: Wiley.

Loeber, R., & Tolan, P. H. (1992). Conduct disorders. In P. H. Tolan & B. Cohler (Eds.), *Handbook of clinical research and practices with adolescents* (pp. 307–331). New York: Wiley.

Moffitt, T. E. (1993). Adolescence-limited and life-course-persistent antisocial behavior: A developmental taxonomy. *Psychological Review, 100,* 674–701.

National Institute of Education. (1978). *Violent schools–safe schools: The Safe Schools Study report to Congress.* Washington DC: U.S. Government Printing Office.

Olweus, D. (1987). Bully/victim among school children. In J. P. Myklebust & R. Ommundsen (Eds.), *Psykologprofesjonen Mot Ar 2000.* Oslo: Universitetsforlaget.

Olweus, D. (1991). Bully/victim problems among school children: Basic facts and effects of a school-based intervention program. In D. Pepler & K. Rubin (Eds.), *The development and treatment of childhood aggression* (pp. 411–446). London: Erlbaum.

Parker, J. G., & Asher, S. R. (1987). Peer relations and later personal adjustment: Are low-accepted children at risk? *Psychological Bulletin, 102,* 357–389.

Patterson, G. R. (1993). Developmental changes in antisocial behavior. In R. DeV. Peters, R. J. McMahon, & V. L. Quinsey (Eds.), *Aggression and violence throughout the life span* (pp. 52–82). London: Sage.

Patterson, G. R., Reid, J. B., & Dishion, T. J. (1992). *Antisocial boys*. Eugene, OR: Castalia.

Rodkin, P. C., Farmer, T. W., Pearl, R., & Van Acker, R. (2000). Heterogeneity of popular boys: Antisocial and prosocial configurations. *Developmental Psychology, 36,* 14–24.

Sampson, R. (1992). Family management and child development: Insights from social disorganization theory. In J. M. McCord (Ed.), *Facts, frameworks, and forecasts: Advances in criminological theory* (Vol. 3, pp. 63–93). New Brunswick, NJ: Transaction.

Sampson, R., & Groves, W. B., (1989). Community structure and crime: Testing social disorganization theory. *American Journal of Sociology, 94,* 774–802.

Sampson, R. J., Raudenbush, S. W., & Earls, F. (1997). Neighborhoods and violent crime: A multilevel study of collective efficacy. *Science, 277,* 918–924.

Selman, R. L., Schultz, L. H., Nakkula, M., Barr, D., Watts, C., & Richmond, J. D. (1992). Friendship and fighting: A developmental approach to the study of risk and prevention of violence. *Development and Psychopathology, 4,* 529–558.

Short, J. F., Jr. (1997). *Poverty, ethnicity, and violent crime*. Boulder, CO: Westview.

Slaby, R. G., & Guerra, N. G. (1988). Cognitive mediators of aggression in adolescent offenders: 1. Assessment. *Developmental Psychology, 26,* 269–277.

Snyder, J., Horsch, E., & Childs, J. (1997). Peer relationships of young children: Affiliative choices and the shaping of aggressive behavior. *Journal of Clinical Child Psychology, 26,* 145–156.

Spergel, I. A. (1995). *The youth gang problem*. New York: Oxford University Press.

Stephens, R. D. (1997). National trends in school violence. In A. P. Goldstein & J. P. Conoley (Eds.), *School violence intervention: A practical handbook*. New York: Guilford.

Straus, M. A., & Gelles, R. J. (1986). Change in family violence from 1975–1985. *Journal of Marriage and the Family, 48,* 476–479.

Thapar, A., & McGuffin, P. (1993). Is personality disorder inherited? An overview of the evidence. *Journal of Psychopathology and Behavioral Assessment, 15,* 325–345.

Tolan, P. H. (1988). Socioeconomic, family, and social stress correlates of adolescents' antisocial and delinquent behavior. *Journal of Abnormal Child Psychology, 16,* 317–332.

Tolan, P. H., Cromwell, R. E., & Brasswell, M. (1986). Family therapy with delinquents: A critical review of the literature. *Family Process, 25,* 619–650.

Tolan, P., & Guerra, N. (1994). *What works in reducing adolescent violence: An empirical review of the field.* Boulder, CO: Center for the Study and Prevention of Violence.

Tolan, P. H., Guerra, N. G., & Kendall, P. C. (1995). Developmental-ecological perspective on antisocial behavior in children and adolescents: Toward a unified risk and intervention framework. *Journal of Consulting and Clinical Psychology, 63,* 579–584.

Tolan, P. H., Guerra, N. G., Van Acker, R., Huesmann, L. R., & Eron, L. D. (1997). Prevalence of psychopathology among urban children: Age, ethnicity, and gender patterns. *Journal of Clinical and Consulting Psychology, 65,* 246–257.

Tracy, P. E., Wolfgang, M. E., & Figlio, R. M. (1990). *Delinquency careers in two birth cohorts.* New York: Plenum.

United States Department of Justice. (1998). *Indicators of school crime and safety: Annual report on school safety.* Washington DC: U. S. Government Printing Office.

Van Acker, R. (1993). Dealing with conflict and aggression in the classroom: What skills do teachers need? *Teacher Education and Special Education, 16,* 23–33.

Van Acker, R., Grant, S. H., & Henry, D. (1996). Teacher and student behavior as a function of risk for aggression. *Education and Treatment of Children, 19,* 316–334.

Vigil, J. D. (1999). Streets and schools: How educators can help Chicano marginalized gang youth. *Harvard Educational Review, 69,* 270–288.

Vigil, J. D., & Yun, S. C. (1996). Southern California gangs: Comparative ethnicity and social control. In R. Huff (Ed.), *Gangs in America* (2nd ed., pp. 139–156). Thousand Oaks, CA: Sage.

Walker, H. M., Colvin, G., & Ramsey, E. (1995). *Antisocial behavior in school: Strategies and best practices.* Pacific Grove, CA: Brooks/Cole.

Walker, H. M., Severson, H. H., & Feil, E. G. (1994). *The Early Screening Project: A proven child-find process.* Longmont, CO: Sopris West.

Wood, M., & Long, N. (1991). *Life space intervention: Talking with children and youth in crisis.* Austin, TX: Pro-Ed.